W9-CXP-503

THE LITTLE BOOK OF
CHRISTMAS

THE LITTLE BOOK OF
CHRISTMAS

Dominique Foufelle

CHRONICLE BOOKS

SAN FRANCISCO

First published in the United States of America in 2017
by Chronicle Books LLC.
First published in France in 2014 by Éditions du Chêne—
Hachette Livre as *Le Petit Livre de Noël*.

Library of Congress Cataloging-in-Publication Data

Names: Foufelle, Dominique, author.
Title: The little book of Christmas / by Dominique Foufelle.
Other titles: Petit livre de Noel. English
Description: San Francisco, CA : Chronicle Books, LLC, 2017.
Identifiers: LCCN 2016040491 | ISBN 9781452161631
Subjects: LCSH: Christmas—Cross-cultural studies. | Christmas decorations.
Classification: LCC GT4985 .F67513 2017 | DDC 394.2663—dc23 LC record available at https://lccn.loc.gov/2016040491

Manufactured in China

MIX
Paper from
responsible sources
FSC
www.fsc.org   FSC™ C136333

Cover design by Lizzie Vaughan
Typeset by Howie Severson
Translated by Deborah Bruce-Hostler

All reproductions in this book are from the private collection of
Éditions du Chêne, except p. 12 © Collection IM / Kharbine-Tapabor;
cover, 63, 77, 79, 83, 85, 97, 115, 122, and 141 © Collection Kharbine-Tapabor.

10 9 8 7 6 5 4 3 2

Chronicle Books LLC
680 Second Street
San Francisco, California 94107
www.chroniclebooks.com

CONTENTS

THE LONG HISTORY OF CHRISTMAS

For many, Christmas is a quintessential family holiday, an occasion to make a special effort, to gather together, to exchange gifts, and, above all, to indulge the children. It is, however, no less and foremost a Christian celebration. It is said that Christmas was first established as a holiday in the fourth century, when Pope Liberius proclaimed the twenty-fifth of December as the official birthdate of Jesus. No precise historical account supports this claim, but when the pope declared the twenty-fifth a holy day, the Church, in effect, was acknowledging the popularity of pagan celebrations that welcomed the winter solstice. The date and the celebration soon became an essential part of Christian custom.

RITUALS AND FEASTING

In the fifth century, the Christian Church introduced observance of Advent. During this season, originally seven, then four weeks long, the faithful prepared themselves to greet the newborn Savior by fasting and praying. Yet they did not neglect to fill their pantries, for Christmas was already synonymous with feasting. In the Middle Ages, pagan traditions, such as the Feast of Fools, survived among holiday pastimes. The Church, which took a dim view of the accompanying exuberant activities, outlawed them.

Around the twelfth century, an enduring custom began in Europe: that of the Yule log or, in French, the *bûche de Noël*. A very large log would be lit at the hearth and had to continue burning for three days. The ritual varied among different regions, but everywhere the log was tended with great care, since the outcome of the year to come depended on its proper burning. In nineteenth-century Europe, wood-burning hearths fell from use, making the Yule log obsolete. Pastry chefs memorialized the custom by creating a holiday cake in the form of a log, still called the *bûche de Noël*.

With the old Yule log glowing in the fireplace, families and neighbors gathered at Midnight Mass, called there by the church bells. Upon returning home, all would sit down to a Christmas Eve repast. Once frugal, through the centuries the Christmas Eve meal became a feast. The roast goose, a vestige of Roman winter solstice celebrations, played a lead role in many countries. The turkey, a newcomer imported from the Americas in the sixteenth century, later dethroned the goose in many places in Europe. Sugary sweets have been gifts since the Middle Ages. The Church imposed a prohibition during Advent against using eggs, butter, or milk in cakes. This did not limit the imagination of pastry cooks in the least; they made spice cakes and sweet biscuits, still essential to the season in Northern Europe.

The fir tree at Christmas recalls pre-Christian traditions. For the ancient Celts and Vikings, the conifer signified the ever green vitality of Nature. Around the seventh century Christians adopted it as a symbol of the Tree of Paradise. In those earlier times, the cut tree, decorated with apples, enlivened public squares in winter. Beginning in the sixteenth century, the fir tree was brought inside to decorate the house for Christmas. Apples and candies were gradually replaced by more and more sophisticated decorations for the tree, many with no religious significance. But candles were used on Christmas trees for centuries, reminding the faithful of the light that they believed the Savior brought to the world. Eventually strings of lights replaced the candles.

Since the late nineteenth century Christmas has become an increasingly secular—in fact, commercial—holiday. This change was marked by a new arrival: Father Christmas, Santa Claus—or Père Noël in France. What inspired this old gentleman was the popular belief that prevailed well before the Christian era that aged figures, sprites, or bearded supernatural beings sometimes bestowed the young or the old with gifts. But more than Celtic forebears or the Scandinavian Julenisse, Father Christmas merged traits from traditions celebrating the December sixth feast day of Saint Nicholas and loaned them to the Anglo-Saxon Santa Claus. Around 1850, the North American illustrator Thomas Nast gave Santa Claus his defining look: rotund silhouette, jovial face,

HEUREUX NOËL.

M.S.B.

and red and white suit. The Coca-Cola Company popularized the image in an ad campaign in 1931.

Until the early twentieth century, gifts were commonly exchanged at New Year's, with children receiving no more than the adults. With the coming of Père Noël or Santa Claus and with the influence of new, large department stores, gift giving grew exponentially. Adults as well as children were given presents on December twenty-fourth or on Christmas Eve, and the ancient tradition of New Year's gifts faded little by little.

ACROSS THE WORLD

Saint Nicholas was never completely eclipsed by Santa Claus. In Northern Europe, the arrival of Saint Nicholas on December sixth still brings joy, even though he is accompanied by a sinister counterpart, known in France as Père Fouettard (Father Whipper). Warmly welcomed in different countries at this season are Christkindel in Alsace, the witch La Befana in Italy, Saint Lucy in Sweden, and Babouschka in Russia. The merrymaking that accompanies their transit earlier in December does not detract from the celebrations of Christmas itself; all is a part of the holiday season that stretches through the month of December and into the early days of January. Religious rites, pagan traditions, and secular customs coexist, just as plans for Christmas Eve and Christmas Day, the decorations, and the meals vary according to region or country. But rarely do those who celebrate Christmas leave out gift giving.

DECEMBER TWENTY-FIFTH

THIS DAY, CHOSEN BY THE CHURCH IN THE
FOURTH CENTURY, COINCIDED WITH PAGAN
CELEBRATIONS OF THE SOLSTICE.

No ancient document gives a precise account of the date of Jesus's birth. This did not bother the early Christians, who gave their attention to the death and Resurrection of their messiah. A passage in the Gospel according to Luke describes the shepherds guarding their sheep near the stable where Mary and the infant Jesus were sheltered. This detail does not argue in favor of the twenty-fifth of December, since in Judea flocks returned from the hills at the end of autumn. But this is the day made official by the Catholic Church in accordance with the decree of Pope Liberius in the year 354. The Church hoped that the ardor of pagan celebrations of the winter solstice, occurring close to this time of year, would translate to a new Christian holy day. The goal was soon fulfilled with acceptance of celebrations of the day; nonetheless, some still refute the inexact decision on when to celebrate the birth of Christ.

ADVENT

BEGINNING ON THE FOURTH SUNDAY
BEFORE CHRISTMAS, CHRISTIANS PREPARE
TO CELEBRATE THE NATIVITY.

When first observed in the fifth century, Advent began on the eleventh of November, Saint Martin's Day. The faithful would fast three times a week until the twenty-fifth of December. Around the ninth century, the Church set the beginning of Advent on the fourth Sunday before Christmas, which also marked the beginning of the liturgical year. Over time, strict observances softened and fasting was no longer required; the faithful prepared to celebrate the birth of Jesus with meditation and with joy.

Many of the customs now associated with the Advent season came from nineteenth-century German Protestants, such as the crown of fir boughs bearing four candles lit sequentially each Sunday during Advent. The Advent calendar marks the days from December first to the twenty-fourth—straying somewhat from the liturgical calendar—with twenty-four paper windows each opened on their proper day. In early versions, each window revealed a holy image; in 1958 in Europe an Advent calendar that held candies appeared. By the popular vote of children, it was a great success. The Advent calendar would come to aid many families in their preparations to greet, no longer Jesus, but Father Christmas.

ISHIAS PROF. — SJOANNES B^{STA}

AVE GRATIA PLENA

1. — EVANGILE DU 1er DIMANCHE DE L'AVENT.

ANGELS

According to tradition, an angel appeared several times in the life of Jesus. They were messengers, as the Greek word *angelos* signifies. The first was the archangel Gabriel, who appeared to a young virgin, Mary of Nazareth, and told her that she would conceive the Son of God. The angel then went to Joseph to dispel his doubts when, having returned from a long journey, he learned that his betrothed was to bear a child.

After the birth of Jesus, a host of angels told nearby shepherds to go to honor the divine child. (These are the angels described in the eighteenth-century French carol *"Des anges dans nos campagnes,"* known in English as "Angels We Have Heard on High.") When King Herod ordered the massacre of all male children under the age of two in Bethlehem, an angel warned Joseph to flee with his family to Egypt. Later in the Gospels, an angel consoled Jesus in the Garden of Gethsemane. An angel announced the Resurrection to Mary Magdalene, and instructed her and the women with her to go tell the other disciples. Traditional Christmas decorations in the form of paper angels are remembrances of these intercessions.

Joyeux Noël

THE ANNUNCIATION

THE ARCHANGEL GABRIEL BROUGHT
TIDINGS TO MARY THAT SHE WAS TO BE A
MOTHER AND YET REMAIN A VIRGIN.

The story of the Annunciation comes from the Gospel according to Luke. A messenger from God, the archangel Gabriel, appeared before the fourteen-year-old Mary of Nazareth. The angel told Mary that she would deliver a son who was to be named Jesus. The young woman, incredulous, answered to Gabriel, "How shall this be done, because I know not man?" The angel said she would conceive by the Holy Spirit and mentioned Mary's cousin Elizabeth, to whom he had announced the coming birth of John the Baptist even though she was past the age of childbearing. Convinced, Mary accepted the honor without seeking the consent of the carpenter Joseph, to whom she was betrothed. In the year 561 Byzantine emperor Justinian named March 25 a holy day celebrating the Annunciation. This tradition came later than 354, when Pope Liberius chose December twenty-fifth to celebrate the birth of Jesus. Interestingly, the two dates are nine months apart.

CHOCOLATERIE D'AIGUEBELLE

L'ANNONCIATION

LES CHEFS D'ŒUVRE DE L'ART RELIGIEUX

POUSSIN

BABOUSCHKA

IT IS SAID THAT THIS INDEFATIGABLE
GRANDMOTHER STILL ROAMS THE STEPPES OF
RUSSIA IN SEARCH OF THE INFANT JESUS.

In Russia, *babouschka* means "grandmother"; the name extends to describe any aged woman. But Babouschka is also the name of a person of legend. She appeared in Russia long before Father Christmas, even if today she plays second fiddle to the old man. Her legend tells that on one icy winter night, Babouschka was drinking tea in the corner beside her hearth when someone rapped on the door of her *isba*, or log cabin. Three bearded men asked to come in to warm themselves for a while. They told her that they were on their way to find the newborn Jesus and invited her to accompany them. Babouschka thought herself much too old for such a journey. But the next morning, full of remorse, she filled a sack with toys and set out to follow them. In every village that she came to, she asked if this was where Jesus was born. As the answer was always "no," she would press on, but not without giving toys to the village children. It is said that her quest continues to this day. Every year Babouschka—whose sack of toys seems inexhaustible—indulges children and delights newborns in honor of the child in Bethlehem.

С НОВЫМ ГОДОМ!

BELLS

The first metal bells used to communicate across long distances date from the Bronze Age. For pagans, their ringing chased away evil spirits. The first Christian bells were used to signal a time to gather. According to tradition, the placing of bells atop churches began in the fourth century, an innovation of Saint Paulinus, Bishop of Nola in Campania in southern Italy. Campania became the source of the word *campana* (bell) in Italian, and *campanile*, or bell tower. Saint Paulinus also originated the idea of sounding the bells at midnight on Christmas Eve to announce the birth of Christ; the bells' peal signaled the time to come to Midnight Mass in a torchlit procession. But in some places, strange bell ringing can be heard on Christmas Eve. In Alsace in France, for example, in the village of Ballersdorf, a church bell hidden in a well by villagers at the approach of invading barbarians can still be heard every year. The same is said of the bell at Zicavo near Ajaccio, on the island of Corsica, thrown by pirates into the sea after they sacked the town.

Joyeux Noël

BETHLEHEM

LONG BEFORE THE BIRTH OF JESUS, THE TOWN WAS
THE BIRTHPLACE OF THE BIBLICAL HERO KING DAVID.

In biblical times, Bethlehem witnessed legendary events. Rachel, known from the Book of Genesis, wife of the patriarch Jacob, died in Bethlehem while giving birth to Benjamin. Her tomb in Bethlehem is still one of Judaism's holy places. The fabled King David, son of Jesse, was born there. After he killed the giant Goliath, he served and later succeeded Saul, becoming king of Judah and Israel. According to the Old Testament, God promised to protect David and his descendants, from whom would come the savior of Israel. Around the seventh century before Christ, the prophet Micah foretold the birth in Bethlehem of "one who will be ruler over Israel"; Christians would see Jesus, descended from David through the lineage of his father, Joseph, as this providential being.

In the second century A.D., the Church officially recognized Bethlehem as the birthplace of Christ. Two centuries later, Emperor Constantine had the Church of the Nativity built over the grotto believed to be the site of the holy birth. Not far from this is the Cave of the Lactation, or Milk Grotto, where Mary took refuge to nurse her child while Joseph prepared for the Flight into Egypt.

MESSAGERIES MARITIMES

L'ÉGLISE DE LA NATIVITÉ, A BETHLÉEM
D'après l'aquarelle de M. G. CARRÉ

THE *BÛCHE DE NOËL* (THE YULE LOG)

THE LOG SOLEMNLY IGNITED ON CHRISTMAS EVE
HAD TO STAY LIT FOR AT LEAST THREE DAYS.

Since the twelfth century in most European countries, the Yule log or *bûche de Noël* would be lit on Christmas Eve. This highly important ritual was performed at nightfall, with all of the household present. The hearth would first be cleaned and then prepared with embers from the last year's Yule log, kept to protect the house from lightning strikes and other calamities. Into the fireplace would be set a log that had been cut before sunrise from a fruit tree, for a good harvest to come. This log would be as big as possible, because it must burn for at least three days, or better, until the New Year. The ritual varied in different regions as to whether father, mother, or youngest child lit the fire. In some places, the log would be sprinkled with warm wine in the hope of a good vintage the next year, or with salt against sorcery, or with milk and honey as a memory of Paradise. As the *bûche de Noël* began to burn, the children were sent to the other side of the room to pray, facing the wall, while the adults set sweet treats on the hearth. The children would be told that these had come from the log itself. This custom faded in the nineteenth century when smaller wood-burning stoves replaced the great fireplaces. The use of a small, decorated log as a centerpiece on the holiday table became its humble replacement.

Heureux Noël

THE *BÛCHE DE NOËL*
(THE YULE LOG CAKE)

WHO INVENTED THIS TRADITIONAL PASTRY?
SEVERAL THEORIES COMPETE.

The iced cake in the form of a log—a dessert that brings the Christmas feast to a close—is a very French tradition. Now known throughout much of the world, it was adopted first in places with ties to France, such as Belgium, Québec, Lebanon, and Vietnam. Its origins without doubt rest in the large log that once was lit on Christmas Eve. The pastry *bûche de Noël* soon followed the disappearance of its wooden counterpart in the nineteenth century. The inventor, however, is in dispute: the apprentice to a chocolate maker in Saint-Germain-des-Prés in Paris conceived this treat in 1834; or, others say, the pastry was born in Lyons in the 1860s. Others believe that Pierre Lacam, the old pastry chef of Charles III, the prince of Monaco, created it in 1898. The traditional *bûche de Noël* cake is filled with buttercream and chocolate shavings, but many now prefer it with a lighter icing.

JOYEUX NOËL

R. GRAND

CANDLES

For people of the Christian faith, Jesus is the Light that illuminates humankind. Candles are lit to commemorate his birth. The color of the tapers varies from country to country: white for purity, red for ardor and radiance, purple for penitence. According to an English custom, a burning candle is set in a window on Christmas Eve to guide the Holy Family on their way to Bethlehem. In Scandinavia, a Christmas candleholder carries three candles to evoke the Trinity. Each of the four candles on the Advent wreath, one is added each Sunday during the four weeks of Advent, has its own significance. The first symbolizes the forgiveness given to Adam and Eve; the second, the Patriarchs' faith in the Promised Land; the third, King David's joy in his alliance with God; the fourth, the Prophets' promise of a world of peace and justice. Popular tradition expresses these symbols in four words: peace, faith, love, and hope.

Joyeux Noël

Nous baisers à tous grande
et pet...

2908.

CAROLS

RELIGIOUS OR SECULAR, THE SONGS KNOWN AS CHRISTMAS CAROLS HAVE ACCOMPANIED THE CELEBRATION FOR CENTURIES.

According to tradition, the first carols were the songs of the angels who hovered over the manger at Bethlehem. These songs inspired canticles, first intoned in Latin in churches, then carols sung in vernacular languages in communities and in homes. Because they announce a happy occasion, Christmas carols are always joyous. Many allude to the stable, the animals, the angels, shepherds, and the Magi. Among the oldest is the French *"Entre le bœuf et l'âne gris"* ("Between the Ox and the Gray Ass" or "Here on the Hay") from the sixteenth century. The eighteenth century saw the origins of other classics from France that were based on old tunes: *"Il est né le divin enfant,"* the Provençal *"Marche des rois mages,"* and *"Des anges dans nos campagnes"* ("Angels We Have Heard on High"). In the nineteenth century, translations of German carols, such as "Silent Night," were added to the repertoire. "Oh Christmas Tree," from a German carol, has become a beloved secular Christmas song for children, a category that includes compositions by twentieth-century American songwriters, such as "Jingle Bells," "White Christmas," and "Rudolph the Red-Nosed Reindeer." *"Petit Papa Noël,"* recorded by French singer Tino Rossi in 1946, has been a popular carol for more than half a century.

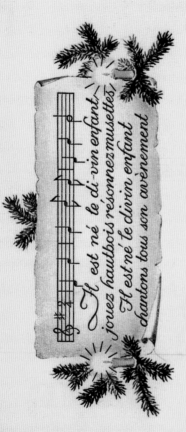

Il est né le di-vin enfant,
jouez hautbois résonnez musettes,
Il est né le divin enfant
chantons tous son avènement

JOYEUX NOËL

THE CHIMNEY

A FAMILY GATHERING PLACE FOR CHRISTMAS
EVE, THE FIREPLACE BECAME THE POINT
OF ACCESS FOR FATHER CHRISTMAS.

In the past, the hearth, sole source of heat in houses
in the countryside, was the gathering place for the
household in the evening. On Christmas Eve, families lit the Yule log, whose sparks represented good
omens. Parents had children believe that the piece of
wood was the source of sweets they would find at the
hearth on Christmas morning. By the early twentieth
century, Santa Claus had replaced the Yule log, and
the fireplace remained a place where gifts were to be
discovered Christmas morning. Children would each
leave a shoe or a slipper along with a snack for Santa
and the reindeer. But why expect Santa to come down
the dangerous and sooty chimney? Indeed, since
he came from the sky, it was convenient for him to
leave his sleigh on the roof. A more realistic answer
could come from ancient times: Father Christmas was
inspired by Saint Nicholas, who was born in the third
century in what is now Turkey and was a benefactor
of poor children. In his time and place, some houses
where he did his good deeds had only an opening in
the roof to serve both as a doorway and the place for
smoke to escape from the household fire. It would
have been this kind of chimney through which one
would see the arrival of good Saint Nicholas.

Veillée de Noël

A CHRISTMAS CAROL

THIS STORY BY CHARLES DICKENS CONTRIBUTED TO THE POPULARITY OF THE CHRISTMAS HOLIDAY IN ENGLAND.

In December 1843, Charles Dickens published his novella *A Christmas Carol*. The English writer told the story of how on one Christmas Eve the old miser Ebenezer Scrooge surrendered to a sense of humanity. Dickens's character owed his transformation to a series of apparitions of his associate's ghost and three tormenting spirits. At the end of this disquieting night, Scrooge makes a decision—extravagant for him—to give his employee a raise. When the book came out, Dickens did not yet enjoy the fame that is now his. A critical and popular success, *A Christmas Carol* made his immense talent evident. Describing a tyrannical employer, Dickens wrote an indictment of the insensitivity of the rich to the suffering of the poor, who were very numerous in Victorian England. The book had a big influence as well on the growing popularity of Christmas festivities that Queen Victoria's husband, Prince Albert, brought from his native Germany. Christmas Day soon became a holiday, in the form of a day off from work.

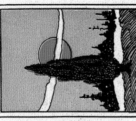

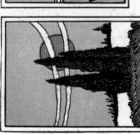

"A merry Christmas and God save you."

Dicken's Christmas Carol.

THE CHRISTMAS EVE REPAST

AFTER GATHERING FOR MIDNIGHT MASS, FAMILY AND NEIGHBORS THEN SHARE A RESTORATIVE FEAST.

In former times, the faithful fasted the day before Christmas. That night, they would take what would often be a long route to church for Midnight Mass. They would emerge from service tired and famished. Hence the custom emerged of serving a late, abundant meal. The rituals vary in different regions, but in Europe pork often plays an important role on the menu. The animal would be slaughtered well ahead of the holiday when it was fat, to ensure that a plentiful larder would be ready for this night. Perishable cuts already would have been eaten, but a black pudding, or blood sausage—*le boudin noir* in French—was obligatory on the Christmas Eve table for a long time. This blood-based cold cut, now considered not so delectable, has disappeared from holiday menus. The French now prefer *boudin blanc*, also an old Christmas custom, born from the imagination of a cook in the seventeenth century who had the idea of putting the ingredients of a hot milk soup, intended as an entrée for the Christmas Eve meal, into gut sausage casings. But in Normandy, the story is told that monks who were obliged to abstain from eating meat invented the *boudin blanc*, or white pudding, to give them the impression that they were eating sausage.

Joyeux Noël

CHRISTMAS GLOBES

A GLASSBLOWER INVENTED THE ROUND GLASS
CHRISTMAS DECORATION IN THE NINETEENTH CENTURY.

In 1858 the Vosges region of Alsace in northeastern France suffered a terrible drought, and the apple crop failed. Since the Middle Ages, it had been the custom in Europe to decorate Christmas boughs with red apples as reminders of the forbidden fruit of the Fall of Man, that is, the Original Sin redeemed by the Messiah. A glassblower at the Goetzenbruck glassworks had the idea to make globes as a substitute, and a tradition that spread across continents was born. Goetzenbruck glassworks, founded in 1721, became the specialist manufacturer of the shiny glass Christmas ball. In the 1950s, they produced around 200,000, small and large, which were exported around the world. Alas, cheaper mass-produced versions quickly rendered the more rarified globes obsolete. The old glassworks stopped making them in 1964, but new production started in 1998 in Meisenthal, in Lorraine, northeastern France. A patriotic counterstory, however, says that in truth, in the history of glass Christmas tree balls, the invention was actually that of a glassblower in Lauscha, Germany, working ten years earlier than the artisan in Vosges.

Bonne Année

CHRISTMAS LIGHTS

CANDLES IN WINDOWS OF THE PAST
PREFIGURED THE SPECTACULAR LIGHTING
DISPLAYS WE SEE TODAY AT CHRISTMAS.

In 1882 Edison Electric Light Company Vice President Edward Hibbard Johnson invented electric Christmas tree lights. At the time, only cities had an electrical system. In 1909, at the Bon Marché department store, the first animated Christmas window display astonished Parisians. But not until the 1950s were towns decorated with lights for the winter holidays. The expansion of Christmas lights went hand in hand with the commercialization of the holiday and the development of tourism. The illumination of the commercial districts and landmarks in cities was copied by smaller towns and later by private households with the use of exterior holiday lights. Themes became less religious, and some non-Christian countries, especially those in Asia, adopted the custom. Holiday lighting displays became an art, and towns competed in lavish arrays. But in recent years, fingers point at the excessive use of electricity and the high cost of these enchantments.

Vesele božične praznike.

THE CHRISTMAS MARKET

IN ALSACE IN FRANCE, THE TRADITION OF THE CHRISTMAS MARKET GOES BACK TO THE FOURTEENTH CENTURY, WHEN IT WAS DEDICATED TO SAINT NICHOLAS.

The great medieval fairs were often associated with the cult of a particular saint. Ever since the fourteenth century, when the first Christmas markets began in Alsace and in Germany, they have been dedicated to the highly venerated Saint Nicholas. The Saint Nicholas market took place around December sixth, a day when gifts were given. In the sixteenth century, the Protestant Reformation condemned the cult of the saints. Saint Nicholas was replaced by the Christkindel, a young girl veiled and dressed in white who personified the infant Jesus; the market of Saint Nicholas was renamed Christkindelmärik, open from the first of December to the twenty-fourth. Since 1570, the city of Strasbourg has been hosting the oldest and largest of these markets. There one can find an abundance of spice breads and other regional sweets, wooden toys, and figures for crèche scenes. Christmas markets did not spread to other regions of France until the 1990s. Most carry on the use of traditional wooden booths and give out warm spiced wine. But the range of articles for sale has expanded, and they no longer are all handmade.

Usages & Costumes alsaciens

CHRISTKINDEL

THE CHRISTMAS ORANGE

WHEN IT WAS STILL RARE, THIS WINTER FRUIT MADE A GIFT THAT WAS VERY MUCH APPRECIATED BY CHILDREN.

The orange tree, which originated in China, was brought to Palestine in the caravans of Arab merchants. From there, Crusaders brought it to Europe. Flowering in winter and needing a warm climate, the tree grew well only on the Iberian Peninsula and in Italy. Farther north, it found refuge in the heated conservatories of royal gardens, and only aristocrats ate oranges. Regular folks didn't know that oranges existed. At the end of the nineteenth century in Europe, when the custom of gift giving for Christmas had spread, the orange was a rare and expensive fruit that was purchased from wandering merchants who came from Spain. Oranges became a luxury for families of modest means who reserved them as a gift for their children. It wasn't until the 1950s that imports democratized the fruit. An orange pierced with cloves, a popular Christmas decoration, recalls those long gone times.

THE CHRISTMAS STOCKING

IN ENGLISH TRADITION, THE STOCKING IS
THE PREFERRED CONTAINER FOR FATHER
CHRISTMAS TO FILL WITH PRESENTS.

On Christmas Eve in England, children don't leave their shoes at the hearth or under the Christmas tree, but instead they leave a large sock. The origin of this custom comes from an episode in the life of the original Saint Nicholas. According to his legend, a widowed neighbor was in despair, unable to provide dowries for her three daughters, who were thereby in danger of having to turn to prostitution to survive. The saintly man, as generous as he was rich, decided to come to their aid, but he wanted his help to be anonymous. At nightfall he left a sack of gold inside some stockings that the young women had left out to dry. He repeated this secret act twice more, to the joy of the family. In the nineteenth century, when Saint Nicholas became Santa Claus, who would visit on the night before Christmas, this legend inspired the custom of leaving a sock for him to fill. At first, children offered a personal sock from their wardrobe, until special Christmas stockings that were much larger and deeper and often homemade became available.

THE CHRISTMAS TREE

ROOTED IN PAGAN PRACTICES, THE TRADITION OF THE
CHRISTMAS TREE CAME VIA NORDIC COUNTRIES.

In ancient times, when evergreen trees represented the regenerative force of Nature, the Celts and the Vikings decorated spruce trees for the winter solstice. Christians adopted the pagan practice around the seventh century, combining it with the December twenty-fifth celebration of the birth of Christ. In the Middle Ages, fir trees set up in public squares for Christmas were decorated with red apples—representing the forbidden fruit to symbolize the Tree of Paradise—and with *oublies*, thin, sugared, unleavened wafers. It was not until the sixteenth century that bringing the trees or their boughs indoors began as a purely Protestant custom of Scandinavian, German, and Alsacian families. In 1738 the wife of Louis XV, the Polish Marie Leszczynska, who had lived in Alsace, brought a Christmas tree to Versailles. Eventually the tradition made it into Catholic homes, spread throughout Europe, and crossed the Atlantic in the nineteenth century. Apples and sweets eventually gave way to more plentiful and elaborate decorations.

Joyeux Noël

SER. 115

THE CHRISTMAS WREATH

THE WREATH OF GREENERY IS A
VESTIGE OF PAGAN CUSTOM.

In 354, when Pope Liberius proclaimed December twenty-fifth as the holy day for celebrating the Nativity, he borrowed from pagan religion—the better to eclipse a pagan festival—by choosing the time of winter solstice celebrations. During this winter period, the ancient Romans decorated their homes with evergreens, symbol of the regenerative power of Nature. The motif of a wheel evoked the immutable cycling of the Sun. Christian tradition took as its own the symbols of evergreen boughs and the wheel to create the wreaths of greens that are made for Christmas. Traditionally placed on a table, the Advent wreath, with four candles lit one by one on the four Sundays before Christmas, marks the meditative but joyous wait for the coming of Jesus. The decorative wreaths hung at doors or windows with a red ribbon symbolizing light first came from Scandinavian tradition and were made throughout Europe before the custom crossed the Atlantic. They have been called "welcome wreaths" because in theory anyone who came to the door would benefit from the law of hospitality. It has become rare, however, that when the table is laid for the Christmas feast, a place setting beyond the head count of guests is set out for "the poor man's plate" as was the custom in the past.

CHRISTMAS IN THE MIDDLE AGES

CROWDS GATHERED FOR CHRISTIAN
CELEBRATIONS AND PAGAN FESTIVALS ALIKE.

In the Middle Ages, Christmas was preceded by a fast that started on Saint Martin's Day (November eleventh) and then another fast that was observed for a final eight days. This sacrifice was duly compensated on Christmas Eve after Midnight Mass, when one would joyfully feast. During the Advent season, theater troupes performed in church squares. Before the twelfth century, they acted out scenes from the Christmas liturgy in sketches that all could understand. These sketches were gradually transformed into plays with more elaborate spectacles inspired by tales from the apocryphal Gospels. The Church judged these plays to be profane and banned them in 1677. Certain popular celebrations of pre-Christian, pagan origin occurred alongside Christian observances. For the Feast of Fools in the days following Christmas—a celebration descended from the festival of Saturn from ancient Rome—social roles were reversed: servants acted as masters, and women and men traded roles. The Feast of the Donkey on January fourteenth commemorated the Flight into Egypt of the Holy Family by having a young woman carry a newborn into the church while the whole congregation brayed "hee-haw!" to punctuate each prayer during Mass. These unorthodox practices did not go for long without condemnation.

SCÈNES DE NOËL.

..... MOYEN-AGE.
Représentation d'un mystère
de Noël chez un châtelain.

VÉRITABLE EXTRAIT DE VIANDE LIEBIG.

Voir au verso.

CHRISTMAS IN ALSACE

PÈRE NOËL REPLACED CHRISTKINDEL, BUT
OTHER TRADITIONS GO ON UNCHANGED.

Children in Alsace in northeastern France are lucky; in December they receive a visit not only from Père Noël but also from other legendary personages who have not yet yielded their position in the region. First, on December sixth, Saint Nicholas passes through. People eat *manneles*, Saint Nicholas bread shaped into little brioche pastry men. Since the fifteenth century, Christkindel has come on Christmas Eve. Oddly enough, this long-haired young girl personifies the Christ Child. Dressed in white, she wears a veil and a crown of candles. Before giving out gifts, she asks Hans Trapp, or Père Fouettard, which children are deserving of gifts. This moment of fright is followed by time spent around the Christmas tree tasting *bredeles* (homemade spice cakes) and mulled wine made with spices and orange peel. On the traditional tiled stove, a vase holds branches from fruit trees cut on December fourth, Saint Barbara's Day, in hopes that they will flower for Christmas. On Christmas Eve, people used to dine on cherry soup; the big meal is served on the twenty-fifth, when the goose stars as *foie gras* (goose liver) and *Ganzeltopf* (roast goose with vegetables).

VIEILLES COUTUMES_*ALSACE*_La Bûche de Noël.

CHRISTMAS IN BELGIUM

FESTIVITIES DO NOT START UNTIL
AFTER CHURCH SERVICES.

As they do in many Northern European countries, in Belgium winter holidays start on the Day of Saint Nicholas. Although December sixth is above all a children's holiday, Belgian students carry on a more boisterous custom in the university cities: the *guindaille*, a drinking spree. To fund their indulgence they go around with tankards in hand taking up a collection. It is said to be prudent to cooperate; otherwise you might be dusted with flour and pelted with eggs by louts. Christmas is more of a family matter. At midnight, citizens of Brussels gather in the main square, where they light candles at the sound of the bells. The Belgians eat after Church services, but unlike the French, they remain faithful to the Christmas blood sausage and wash it down with beer. Breweries have made special Christmas blends since the beginning of the nineteenth century. Dessert, depending on region, means *cougnous* or *cougnolles*, cookies in the form of Baby Jesus, or *boukètes*, thick buckwheat crêpes garnished with raisins and apple slices.

BLEU RICHTER

Nuit de Noël (Flandre)

CHRISTMAS IN CANADA

REJECTED BY THE FIRST PROTESTANT COLONISTS, THE HOLIDAY SNOWBALLED IN THE NINETEENTH CENTURY.

Among the first colonists to settle in Canada, many were Puritans of the Protestant faith who did not celebrate the Christmas holiday, a Catholic invention that was too festive for their taste. Catholic colonists from France, by contrast, imported the celebrations and traditions of their homeland. In 1781, the English garrison at Sorel in Québec borrowed the tradition of the Christmas tree brought by soldiers of German origin. It took until the nineteenth century for holiday observances to spread in the country, and until the 1920s for the Christmas tree to be brought indoors. As was the case in Europe and the United States, Père Noël and Santa Claus arrived at the end of the nineteenth century. Among the citizens of Québec, where Catholicism exercised considerable influence into the mid twentieth century, celebration of Noël began with Christmas Eve. Thus, on December twenty-fourth families gathered to sing carols and tell stories before going together to Midnight Mass. Afterward, they returned home for mincemeat pie. On most tables in Canada the turkey reigns for the Christmas Eve repast; the bird is native to the Americas, where they are raised in abundance.

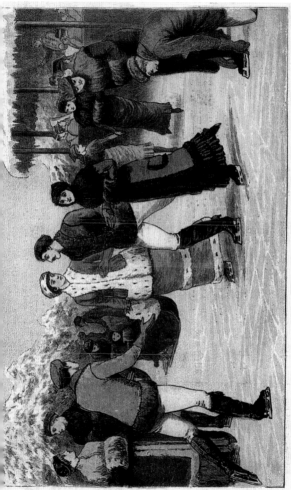

CHRISTMAS IN CANADA

FROM THE PICTURE BY TOWNELEY GREEN

CHRISTMAS IN ENGLAND

THE FESTIVITIES IN ENGLAND ARE ALL THE MERRIER
WHEN THE BRITISH GET A LONGER HOLIDAY.

In England, preparations for Christmas begin with Advent and the writing of Christmas cards. England is the world champion in the sending of Christmas cards, a tradition since the nineteenth century. Many use received cards as Christmas decorations for their homes. A week before Christmas, carolers gather on street corners to sing as a means of collecting donations for charity. On Christmas Eve, Santa Claus leaves gifts in Christmas stockings, large socks that children leave near the Christmas tree. The next day, after Christmas services, the meal must include turkey stuffed with sausage and onion, as well as Christmas pudding, a steamed cake with custard cream. In some families, children must wait until after the meal to open their presents. They used to wait until the next day, Boxing Day (referring to gifts in a box), also a day off from work. The tradition was to spend the day giving gifts to the less fortunate. Now many attend a game of rugby or soccer, or go shopping at sales. If the twenty-fifth or twenty-sixth falls on a weekend, not to worry; holiday leaves are given on the weekdays that follow.

CHICORÉE AU DERNIER BAMBOU
CASIEZ-BOURGEOIS

XVIIIème Siècle
ANGLETERRE *:* La Veillée de Noël

CHRISTMAS IN FINLAND

IN THE HOMELAND OF FATHER CHRISTMAS, THIS HOLIDAY IS THE MOST IMPORTANT OF THE YEAR.

In Finland, decorations, gatherings, and holiday visits are underway at the beginning of December. On the twenty-fourth at noon, the "peace of Christmas" is proclaimed on the great square of the old capital at Turku. In a ceremony aired on radio and television, the mayor reads a declaration that dates from the Middle Ages. This marks a day of détente, a cessation of any hostilities for the duration, accompanied by rice pudding, warm wine, and saunas. At nightfall, Finnish people go to cemeteries to place candles at the graves of loved ones. Christmas Eve dinner usually involves a roasted ham with mustard. According to legend, one eats pork for Christmas so that the animal's oinking cannot disturb the sleep of the infant Jesus. At midnight, Father Christmas parks his sleigh by the front door, knocks, and asks whether there are any good children in the house. The answer is of course "yes," and children disguised as elves help him hand out presents.

VÉRITABLE EXTRAIT DE VIANDE LIEBIG.

Voir l'explication au verso.

CHRISTMAS IN GERMANY

WHETHER THEY ARE ABOUT PAGAN CUSTOMS OR OVERINDULGING, TRADITIONS HAVE BECOME RESPECTABLE.

In Germany, Christmas is called *Weihnachten*, or "holy nights." The use of the plural recalls pre-Christian times when the Germanic tribes considered all the nights in December sacred. At the winter solstice, they sacrificed boars or horses to Wotan, the god of war and of lightning, who was given the title of Unvanquished Sun. The night of December twenty-fourth is called *Heilige Abend*, or Holy Night. Christmas preparations in Germany start at the beginning of December, before the arrival of Saint Nicholas, whose feast day is December sixth. Small traditional cakes called *Weihnachtsplätzchen* are made, including *Gebildbrote*, cakes that are shaped like stars or animals, such as the ones once sacrificed to Wotan. The most spectacular is the *Hexenhaus*, a gingerbread house that re-creates the witch's house from the story of Hansel and Gretel recounted by the Brothers Grimm. The *Christstollen*, made with raisins and almond paste, finishes off the Christmas Eve meal. The Christmas tree, tended with great care, also recalls pagan beliefs: the ancient German peoples believed that Yggdrasil—the World Tree—an enormous ash tree that always stayed green, held up the whole universe.

XV eme Siècle — ALLEMAGNE ※ Le repas de Noël

CHRISTMAS IN HOLLAND

CHRISTMAS IS CELEBRATED QUIETLY, BECAUSE MORE
ATTENTION IS GIVEN TO THE DAY OF SAINT NICHOLAS.

In the Netherlands, December twenty-sixth is a day off
from work, along with the twenty-fifth, a time for celebrating with the family. But the most anticipated festival,
though not a day off, is the sixth of December, the Day
of Saint Nicholas. On the third Saturday of November,
Saint Nicholas brings a boat ashore to a different port
each year. His party, having come from Spain, travels in
the Netherlands for three weeks. Nothing in the life of
this saint supports this place of origin; this detail came
from the imagination of the writer Jan Schenkman, who
published a successful children's book in 1850, *Saint
Nicholas and His Servant*.

TAPIOCA-LOUIT

XVIIème Siècle ∗ HOLLANDE ∗ Nuit de Noël.

CHRISTMAS IN ITALY

NEITHER SANTA LUCIA NOR LA BEFANA
HAS BEEN ECLIPSED BY SANTA.

In Italy, celebrations begin on December eighth, when processions are held on the feast day of the Immaculate Conception of Mary and the Advent season begins. Christmas crèches, or *presepi* (mangers)—Nativity scenes—an Italian invention, are installed in homes and in public places. In the north of the country, Santa Lucia is still celebrated on December thirteenth. The Sicilian martyr, accompanied by her donkey, Tobias, and her helper, Gastaldo, distributes gifts to children. Many families, however, have adopted Babbo Natale, Father Christmas. One of the treats that people snack on while waiting for him is *panettone*. Created in Milan in 1490, this sweet brioche bread with candied fruit is popular throughout Italy. December twenty-sixth is consecrated to Santo Stefano, Christendom's first martyr. This holiday is spent taking walks and visiting. Some children, although it's rare these days, must wait until the night of January fifth or sixth, at Epiphany, to receive their gifts. Riding on her broom, the good witch La Befana brings them. In the shoe of little holy terrors, however, she leaves a lump of coal, which these days is actually a black licorice candy.

Buon Natale

CHRISTMAS IN NORWAY

THE VIKINGS INVITE THEMSELVES TO THE CELEBRATION
BY MEANS OF VERY OLD TRADITIONS.

Abandoned by city folk, ancient customs remain alive in the Norwegian countryside. One of these bygone customs is to start holiday preparations by giving the house a thorough cleaning. Another is the tradition of brewing *juleøl*, a strong, amber Christmas beer that dates back to the Vikings, who clinked their drinking horns in honor of the gods Odin, Froy, and Njord. Pork is served for Christmas because at Yule, the pagan winter festival, a pig was sacrificed to Froy. On Christmas Eve, a bowl of gruel is offered to the farm's elf to stay in his good graces; a wreath of grains is left outside for the birds; and the farm animals are given extra feed for the holiday. No one must stay alone at this time, so hospitality is offered to isolated neighbors. Another country custom is to circle the Christmas tree singing songs. After the traditional meal and gift giving by Santa, the family refrains from clearing the table of leftovers from the feast, since the departed, it is said, leave their graves this night and will be angry if nothing is left for them to eat when it's their turn.

LA NOËL EN NORVÈGE.

CHRISTMAS IN PROVENCE

THE SYMBOLISM OF NUMBERS IS NOTEWORTHY
IN PROVENÇAL TRADITIONS.

On December fourth, Saint Barbara's Day, it is customary to put grains of wheat in three saucers of water with some damp cotton to germinate the seeds. If the sprouts grow straight, the year will be prosperous, and the greens that are produced are added to the crèche decorations. In Provence, in southeastern France, artisans have excelled in the art of the *santoun* or *santon* ("little saint"), which are small clay figures. Since the end of the eighteenth century, Provençal crèches feature not only the place and protagonists of the Nativity but also the villagers who came to give homage to the Christ Child. All the traditional trades and community roles are represented, including inescapable characters such as the village simpleton Lou Ravi (the Beguiled One), with his arms up in the air. The big holiday meal is served on Christmas Eve before Midnight Mass. The table settings are arranged over three white tablecloths with three candleholders and the three saucers of sprouted wheat. (The number three evokes the Trinity.) Seven meatless dishes to recall the Seven Sorrows of Mary are served with thirteen small bread rolls, which correspond to Jesus and the Apostles at the Last Supper. Thirteen desserts are put on the table after Midnight Mass, but they stay there until the twenty-seventh of December, the feast day of John the Baptist.

COUTUMES DE NOËL. — Au village des Baux, en Provence, avant la messe de minuit, a lieu la procession de l'agneau que bergers et pastourelles offrent à l'Enfant Jésus. Cérémonie pittoresque qui se déroule au son des fifres et des tambourins et attire chaque année de nombreux spectateurs. (Composition de Duhamel.)

CHRISTMAS IN RUSSIA

THE RUSSIAN ORTHODOX CHRISTMAS IS CELEBRATED ON JANUARY SEVENTH, FOLLOWING THE JULIAN CALENDAR.

Russia adopted the Gregorian calendar, but the Orthodox Church adheres to the ancient Julian calendar for holy days. Christmas is celebrated on the night of January sixth or seventh, which is also the ideal time for divination if one believes surviving pagan traditions. It is customary to fast until the appearance of the first star in the sky, in memory of the Star of Bethlehem. After celebration of the Divine Liturgy, singers carry a star on a pole through the streets; when they knock on a door, they must be let in. Their songs, the *koliadki*, invoke the pagan god Koliada and were long forbidden unless the singers changed the lyrics to what the Church allowed. For the Christmas meal, the table is strewn with hay in honor of the manger of the Nativity, then covered with a white tablecloth. It is traditional to serve twelve dishes, the only obligatory one being *kutya* (or *koutia*), a sweet pudding of boiled grain and dried fruit. During the night, Ded Moroz—Grandfather Frost—comes with his daughter Snegourotchka to help give out presents, or according to what some others believe, it is old Babouschka who leaves gifts. Russian Christmas is the start of twelve days of festivities, the *siatki*, until the nineteenth of January, when the Baptism of Christ is celebrated.

LA NOËL POPULAIRE EN RUSSIE.

CHRISTMAS IN SOUTH KOREA

FOR THE UNMARRIED, CHRISTMAS EVE
CORRESPONDS TO VALENTINE'S DAY.

About half of the South Korean population practices a religion, and the majority of these are Buddhists. Christmas, of course, is not a cultural tradition in Korea. Korean Christians, including many Protestants, do celebrate Christmas in the family as a religious holiday. December twenty-fifth is not a holiday from work, but with westernization, streets are lit up at the end of the year and commercial fervor is in full swing. South Koreans have given a new twist to Christmas Eve, turning it into a kind of Valentine's Day. Couples go out to restaurants and nightclubs and give each other small gifts. For those who haven't found a soul mate, giant speed-dating events are organized in cities. Individuals congregate, women in red on one side, men in white on the other. At a signal, they approach each other, hoping to find someone compatible to pass the evening with. For gatherings and gifts, families wait until New Year's, which is celebrated twice, once according to the solar calendar and once according to the lunar calendar.

CHRISTMAS IN SPAIN

In this still strongly Catholic country, the spiritual celebrations of Christmas have not lost their appeal. Joyous
customs mark the end of the year and the beginning
of the new. Celebrations begin on December twenty-
second with the drawing of the *Sorteo de Navidad*. An
institution since 1812, this national lottery is considered
one of the world's biggest according to wins and play-
ers: 98 percent of Spaniards try their luck. On the evening of the twenty-fourth, families gather early to go to
Midnight Mass, called the "Rooster's Mass" because it
finishes around five in the morning. December twenty-
eighth is Holy Innocents' Day, in memory of the infants
massacred by Herod's order. Despite its tragic aspect,
the festival resembles April Fools' Day, with paper dolls
being stuck to people's backs. Children wait for January
sixth, when the Magi—the Three Wise Men—bring gifts.
In this way, many Spanish snub Father Christmas and
keep the tradition of celebrating Epiphany.

LA FÊTE DE NOËL EN ANDALOUSIE. — LES DANSES DE LA NUIT DE NOËL À SÉVILLE.

CHRISTMAS IN SWEDEN

On the first Sunday of Advent in Sweden, people put a wreath on their door and set stars, Christmas figures, and burning candles in their windows to welcome *Jul Tomte*, the Christmas elf. Gifts are enhanced with cards bearing a few lines composed by the giver. But the greatest attention is given to honoring Saint Lucy, who is linked to light and celebrated on the thirteenth of December. Many legends surround this saint, who died a martyr in 304. One tells that she would bring food at night to Christians hiding in the catacombs, having freed her hands by wearing a wreath of candles. Such candle wreaths are found in Sweden in December, worn by young girls dressed all in white who go through the streets on the saint's day, followed in procession by boys wearing tall pointed hats. Like Saint Lucy herself, the girls give away saffron cakes. Christmas festivities finish up on Saint Knut's Day, the thirteenth of January. The Vikings used to perform sacrifices on this same date. Now people in Sweden prefer to dance around the Christmas tree before taking it down on this day, but first they eat the cookies and candies that decorated it.

Quelques aspects des cérémonies traditionnelles qui se déroulent chaque année en Suède à l'occasion des Fêtes de Noël. (Voir *Promenades*, p. 9.) (Composition de Beauce.)

THE CRÈCHE

THE "LIVING CRÈCHE" OF THE THIRTEENTH
CENTURY LATER SHRANK IN SIZE BUT
MULTIPLIED ITS CAST OF CHARACTERS.

The word *crèche* originally described a manger, a feeding trough for livestock. According to tradition, Mary placed her newborn son in the hay of a manger to warm him; *crèche* came to signify the scene of the Nativity. Saint Francis of Assisi created the first Christmas crèche in 1223, when he prompted townspeople in Italy to recreate the Nativity scene. This inspired Christians in many churches to create a living crèche for Midnight Mass. Smaller Nativity scenes made of terra-cotta or wood, an innovation attributed to the Jesuits, appeared in the sixteenth century. In the next century, the family crèche became fashionable among aristocratic families in Naples, with the holy figures in sumptuous dress. This tradition had spread to France by the French Revolution, when public crèches were outlawed. Crèches in Provence in the South of France are distinguished by their profusion of characters, or *santon* figures. Jesus, Mary, Joseph, the angels, ox, ass, shepherds, and the Magi are joined by figures from village life who represent traditional trades. All the decorations and *santons* would be installed in the crèche scene during Advent, except the manger, which was left empty until midnight of Christmas Eve, when the figure of the infant Jesus would be added.

DECORATIONS

CHRISTMAS DECORATIONS HAVE GROWN IN VARIETY,
BUT THE GREAT CLASSICS REMAIN INDISPENSABLE.

Decorated Christmas trees have been placed in church squares since the Middle Ages. At first the adornments were edible: nuts, cookies, sweets, and above all apples, symbols of the lost Paradise and ancestors of glass Christmas balls. Around the fifteenth century, French artisans invented "angel's hair," tinsel made of fine strips of silver paper, which is now produced from strips of metallic foil. To brighten the tree even more, candles were added in the next century; tradition calls for twelve, one for each month of the year. The introduction of the clip candleholder in 1890 addressed the problem of how to safely attach candles to the tree. But the fire hazard persisted until the 1950s, when strings of electric lights became affordable. Christmas trees are decorated with paper or wood figures such as Santa, angels, elves, and snowflakes, with the Star of Bethlehem at the top. Around the house, decorations remain mostly traditional: the Yule log, evergreens, pinecones, holly, the wreath, and, for the faithful, a large candle that must keep burning through the night.

88

Joyeux Noël

ELVES

THESE MINIATURE HUMANOIDS WITH MISCHIEVOUS DISPOSITIONS ARE SANTA'S HELPERS.

Since ancient times, elves have been well known among Germanic, Celtic, and Gallo-Roman peoples. They lived in the forests, although at first they had been aquatic creatures. Depending on region and era, they have been called elves, dwarfs, korrigans, trolls, or gnomes. Very short in stature, usually wearing a hat, and endowed with magical powers, elves all have a mischievous temperament they indulge at the expense of humans. People once took great care to treat them with consideration and give them food, because they could either protect the household or rain down catastrophes on it. Beliefs became tales, and elves nowadays are thought to be benevolent. The idea of elves being associated with Santa came about in Scandinavia in the twentieth century. Eleven months of the year, the elves make toys and take care of reindeer. On the first of December they leave the North Pole and scatter across the world. Some traditions say that they tease children and parents, or they decide which children have been well behaved enough to receive presents. For a few years, a new tradition was the rage in Canada: the search for Christmas gnomes.

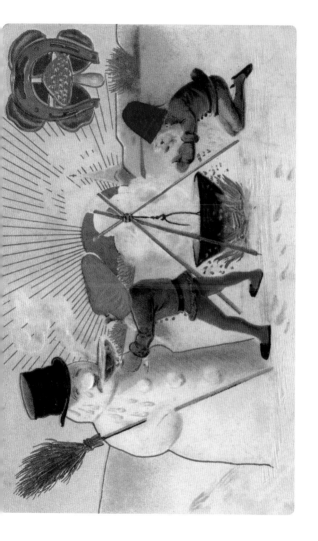

FATHER CHRISTMAS'S COSTUME

A BLEND OF MANY LEGENDS, FATHER CHRISTMAS OVER TIME SETTLED INTO HIS CHARACTERISTIC TRAITS.

In the nineteenth century, Dutch immigrants brought Saint Nicholas to the United States. Crossing the Atlantic brought a change of color to his outfit: once red, it became, for a time, green. In 1823, the New York minister Clement Clarke Moore anonymously published the poem "A Visit from Saint Nicholas" in a newspaper. With the first line of verse, "'Twas the night before Christmas," the preacher affirmed December twenty-fourth as the time for the arrival of Saint Nicholas. He described a small, plump, smiling old man with the identifying characteristics of Father Christmas—the sleigh drawn by reindeer and the fur-lined suit and hood—but gave no hint of the color of his clothes. In Europe, Father Christmas was described as tall and slender, like his predecessor Saint Nicholas, and clothed in a light brown costume, like the robes of a monk, or dressed in purple, like liturgical vestments, or green, or blue. In 1863, the political cartoonist Thomas Nast took up the figure of the big-bellied old fellow. Nast worked on the subject for thirty years, first giving him a brown costume; he finally made it bright red, the color that would become definitive.

FATHER CHRISTMAS'S ORIGINS

BEFORE SAINT NICHOLAS EVOLVED INTO
FATHER CHRISTMAS, OTHER OLD BEARDED
FELLOWS GAVE OUT GIFTS.

Saint Nicholas is generally regarded as the predecessor of Father Christmas. The two venerable old gentlemen share common traits: their advanced age, white beard, and long coat. The Nordic character Father Christmas, however, could have some even older ancestors based in pagan beliefs and legends. One could be the Viking deity Odin, a bearded old god who did not really seem like a soft touch but would come down from Valhalla to give gifts to children. The Gallo-Celtic deity Gargan, who like Jesus was conceived by a virgin, played the same role among the Gauls. The Scandinavian elf Julenisse could also be in the family tree of Father Christmas; he came from the Nisse, little people with white beards and red caps. Julenisse became the Christmas gift giver in Scandinavia in the mid-nineteenth century. According to a Russian legend, Father Christmas was a fourth Wise Man who lived too far away to arrive in time with the Magi; he gave up the journey and decided to devote himself to the noble task of indulging children.

FATHER JANUARY

OLDER THAN FATHER CHRISTMAS, FATHER
JANUARY ALSO USES THE CHIMNEY, BUT
ON THE LAST NIGHT OF THE YEAR.

Despite the popularity of Father Christmas or Santa
Claus since the early twentieth century, Father
January, who was also responsible for indulging children, was still coming to the region of Burgundy in
east-central France as late as the 1930s. Knowing that
Father January did not like them to be greedy, children
would ask for only one present. On the night of January
thirty-first, they would leave a shoe at the hearth,
because like Father Christmas, Father January would
come down the chimney. But watch out; he, too, might
arrive with Père Fouettard (Father Whipper) dragging a
sack full of whips! In the morning, children would find a
toy in their shoe and often candies as well. They would
gather up their gifts and then leave on a tour of the
village, where all the children wished a happy New Year
to family, friends, and wealthier citizens, who would
give them a coin or two. Some families still keep the
tradition of Father January, even though he is less generous than Father Christmas.

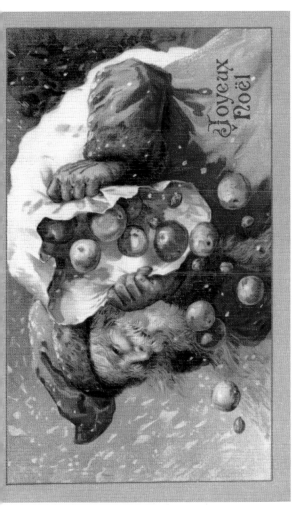

Joyeux Noël

THE FEAST DAY OF SAINT NICHOLAS

THIS MERRY GATHERING IS STILL DEAR TO THE HEARTS OF MANY PEOPLE IN NORTHERN EUROPE.

Saint Nicholas's feast day, celebrated since the tenth century, is the sixth of December. Parts of France, Belgium, the Netherlands, and other areas north and east remain faithful to him. Inspired by the legendary Bishop Saint Nicholas of Myre, this friend of children is called Sinterklaas in Flemish, Santaklos or Nikolaus in German, and Santa Claus in English. Saint Nicholas's traditional appearance includes a long white beard, a white vestment with a long red cloak, a bishop's mitre on his head, and a crosier in his hand. On the night of the fifth of December, children leave a shoe with a carrot intended for the saint's donkey on the hearth or at the door; in the morning, they find sweets in its place. On the sixth, the old gentleman has a busy day visiting schools and going through the streets. Unfortunately, he is accompanied on his tours by Père Fouettard (Father Whipper), who shakes his cat-o'-nine-tails at naughty children.

VIEILLES COUTUMES — ALSACE — La St Nicolas.

GARLANDS

IT'S HARD TO IMAGINE A CHRISTMAS TREE
WITHOUT GARLANDS—THANKS, THE STORY
GOES, TO SOME WITTY SPIDERS.

A German legend tells a charming version of the origins of Christmas garlands. A woman cleaned and decorated her home in preparation for the coming of Father Christmas. As soon as she went to bed, spiders spun their webs over the Christmas tree. Father Christmas found that their silk worked quite well for hanging presents on the tree, but for a more decorative look, he turned the spiderwebs into threads of gold and silver. Ever since, garlands have been a part of traditional decorations for Christmas. Purists even slip a small live spider among the tree boughs. This story has been told since the first mention of Father Christmas in the nineteenth century. In 1882, Edward Hibbard Johnson, vice president of the Edison Electric Light Company, invented Christmas lights with colorful electric bulbs. He was able to light his own Christmas tree because he lived in one of the few sections of New York with electrical service. The Edison Company did not commercialize his invention until 1901.

GIFTS

THE CUSTOM OF GIVING CHRISTMAS GIFTS DID NOT BECOME COMMON UNTIL THE NINETEENTH CENTURY.

The shepherds and the Magi, the first to greet the newborn Jesus, did not arrive empty handed. Their gifts were the precursors of Christmas presents. In the fourth century, the Church set December twenty-fifth as the birthdate of Jesus; besides being a religious celebration, Christmas Eve became a time for festivities. Since the Middle Ages, food supplies were put aside to set a generous feast table, and children were treated to sweets. But toys as gifts did not come into fashion until the nineteenth century, when Christmas celebrations became a family event, and among the affluent it became common for presents to appear piled high under the Christmas tree after a visit from Santa. Adults, who before had more often exchanged gifts for the New Year, also came to enjoy exchanging Christmas presents wrapped in bright-colored paper and tied with curly ribbons.

Voir au verso.

GREETING CARDS

IN THE NINETEENTH CENTURY, THE
ENGLISH POPULARIZED ILLUSTRATED
CARDS SENT FOR THE HOLIDAYS.

On the first of May in 1840, the "Penny Black" stamp with the likeness of Queen Victoria, the first British postage stamp for the public postal system, came off the presses. After its introduction, the sender of a letter rather than the recipient paid the postman—a more courteous arrangement. Around the same time, the development of lithography, which enabled reproduction of extensive multiple prints, popularized the use of illustrated cards. Thanks to these two innovations, the tradition of sending cards in December with wishes for a joyous Christmas season began and by the end of the nineteenth century had spread to other countries. Eventually the practice was extended to sending New Year's greetings. For some, custom calls for writing a long holiday letter to faraway friends and for visiting those nearby. Many who judge this custom as too troublesome regard the greeting card as a simpler alternative.

Noël

Souvenir

DE CANNES

HOLLY

In the Gospel according to Matthew, Herod the Great,
who reigned in Judea during the childhood of Jesus,
heard the priests report the birth at Bethlehem of one
said to be the King of the Jews. When Herod failed
to find the newborn, he ordered the killing of all male
children under the age of two in the district in order
to retain absolute power. Warned of the danger, Mary,
Joseph, and their son departed to take refuge in Egypt.
On their way, they saw soldiers and hid in a thicket of
holly that miraculously spread its branches to conceal
them. In thanks to the plant, Mary blessed it and vowed
that it would always stay green. To this day, Christmas
wreaths and decorations include holly.

JOSEPH

Only the Gospels of Matthew and Luke give an account of Joseph. Details differ, but both Gospels describe the adoptive father of Jesus as a descendant of King David. The evangelists agree that Joseph was a carpenter and that he was much older than Mary, who was only fourteen when they were betrothed. The Protoevangelium of James presents Joseph as a widower and father of several children. The Orthodox Church accepts this account, but the Roman Catholic Church, which considers the Protoevangelium apocryphal, prefers to describe Joseph as consecrated to God and remaining chaste all his life. Whatever the case, he was not an object of devotion until the thirteenth century. His popularity grew thereafter, and in 1621 his feast day on the nineteenth of March became a holy day of obligation, when the faithful are required to attend Mass. Louis XIV made the day a holiday in celebration of the birth of his first son in 1661. In 1870, Pope Pius IX declared Saint Joseph the patron saint of the Universal Church. His successor, Leo XIII, gave Joseph the title "holy patron of fathers and laborers." Joseph has represented an ideal of fatherly devotion in popular imagination for centuries. The Church emphasizes his modesty as an honest artisan; in 1955 Pope Pius XII gave Joseph another feast day, the first of May.

Charpentiers

Ardoisiers

SAINT   JOSEPH

JOYEUX NOËL!

IN MANY LANGUAGES THERE ARE MANY WORDS FOR *CHRISTMAS*, WITH A DIVERSITY OF LINGUISTIC ORIGINS.

The word *Noël* derives from the Latin *natalis*, which means "born." The French word replaced the Old French *Nael* in the twelfth century. The same root is found in the Italian *Natale*, in *Nadal* in the Occitan and Catalán languages of the South of France and Spain, *Nadau* in Provençal, the Portuguese *Natal*, and even *Nedeleg* in the Celtic Breton language. The Spanish *Navidad* comes from the ecclesiastical Latin term *Nativitas*, the "Nativity." The Romanian word *Crăciun* derives from another Latin word, *creatio*, or "creation." The English word *Christmas* translates as "Christ's Mass," which has the same meaning as *Kerstmis* in Dutch. In Japanese there is the adapted word *Kurisumasu*, in Hindi *Krisamasa*, in Persian *Krysmas*, and *Kirihimete* in Maori. In German the word *Weihnacht* combines *weih* for "sacred" and *Nacht* for "night." The plural of this word became *Fröhliche Weihnachten*, which refers to the cycle of twelve nights from December twenty-fifth until Epiphany and means "Merry Christmas" or "Joyeux Noël." The same idea occurs in the Czech *Vánoce* and the Slovakian *Viánoce*, both of which contain *noc*, meaning "night." Scandinavian languages have the word *Jul* ("Yule"), of pre-Christian pagan origin, designating the celebration of the winter solstice.

LETTERS TO SANTA

EVEN WITHOUT A STAMP OR AN ADDRESS, LETTERS TO SANTA ALWAYS REACH THEIR DESTINATION.

The custom of writing to Santa spread in the 1950s. At first the letters were considered undeliverable and were rejected at post offices. This upset two postal workers in France, Odette Messager and Magdeleine Homo, who assumed the tasks of opening the letters and answering them. In 1962 the director of Postes, Télégraphes et Téléphones, Jacques Merette, decided to create the Secrétariat du Père Noël and had a response card designed, with illustrations by René Chag and text composed by Merette's sister, the eminent child psychoanalyst Françoise Dolto. The card said: "My dear child, your kind letter made me very happy. I am sending you my portrait. You see, the mailman found me; he is very clever. I've received many requests. I'm not sure whether I can bring you what you ask for. I'll try, but I am old and sometimes I make mistakes. You must forgive me. Be good, work hard. A big hug, Père Noël." In 1967 the Secrétariat du Père Noël was moved to Libourne in southwestern France. Costs of the service led the authorities to close the program the next year. This decision provoked an outcry, and the office was reopened in 1969. Compared to about two thousand in 1962, letters to Père Noël now surpass one million. Since 1998 Père Noël also has been accepting e-mail.

THE LITTLE PREACHERS

IN A CHURCH IN ROME, CHILDREN COME TO
SING PRAISES TO THE SANTO BAMBINO.

In the fifteenth century, a Franciscan friar carved a statue of the Christ Child from olive wood that came from the Garden of Gethsemane near Jerusalem. According to legend, he had no money to buy paint, but while he took a nap, an angel painted the face of Jesus. Seeing the miracle, the congregation sent the statue, which they called the Santo Bambino—the Holy Child—to Rome. Alas, during the sea crossing, a storm sent the statue overboard, and a new miracle unfolded: the statue beached itself at Livorno, where people were waiting for the boat. Installed in the Basilica of Santa Maria in Aracoeli in Rome, the Santo Bambino multiplied its miracles. The faithful covered it with votive offerings. During the eight days after Christmas (called the *octave*), a small stage was set up in front of the statue where young children took turns singing its praises. These little preachers came from all over Italy and drew large crowds as they gave sermons with great conviction. This unique custom endured until the beginning of the twentieth century.

ROME. — LES PETITS PRÉDICATEURS DE NOËL.

THE MAGI

The Gospel according to Matthew mentions that the
newborn Christ was presented to the Wise Men who
came from the East. The Evangelist did not call them
kings, nor did he specify their names. Since the fifth
century, the Church fixed the date of their arrival in
Bethlehem as the sixth of January, called Epiphany.
According to the *Book of the Cave of Treasures*, written
in the fifth or sixth century in the Syriac language, the
Magi watched for the Star of Bethlehem from Mount
Nud in Persia. Christian iconography has been giving
them crowns since the ninth century. In the twelfth
century, the chronicler and archbishop Jacobus de
Voragine referred to them as the Three Magi Kings in
his *Golden Legend*. He borrowed from the Evangelist
where Matthew describes the three gifts they offered
to the infant Jesus: gold, symbol of royalty; frankin-
cense, ancient ritual substance that marked the divine
essence of the newborn; and myrrh, a fragrant resin
used to embalm the dead, alluding to the mortal aspect
of Christ. Voragine also gave the Magi names: Caspar,
Balthasar, and Melchior. Each represented one of the
three ages of man, adolescence, maturity, and old age,
as well as the diversity of peoples, one African, one
European, and one Asian.

MARY

Mary is first mentioned in the Gospels when the archangel Gabriel visits her at the time of her miraculous conception of Jesus. She then only appears in her son's company. Before he dies, Jesus entrusts his mother to his disciple John, leading us to believe that by then she was a widow. Apocryphal texts are more generous with details about her childhood and the life of the Holy Family. Mary has been the subject of many theological controversies. Christians believe in the doctrine of the Virgin Birth, but unlike Catholics and Orthodox Christians, Protestants reject the doctrine of Mary's perpetual virginity. Citing passages of the New Testament that mention the brothers and sisters of Jesus, Protestants do not believe that Mary remained a virgin all her life. Only Catholics accept the dogma of the Immaculate Conception, which teaches that Mary herself was conceived free of the taint of original sin. Belief in the Assumption of Mary, according to which the Virgin rose directly to Heaven without experiencing death or decay, led to a holy day instituted in the eighth century but only becoming official dogma in 1950.

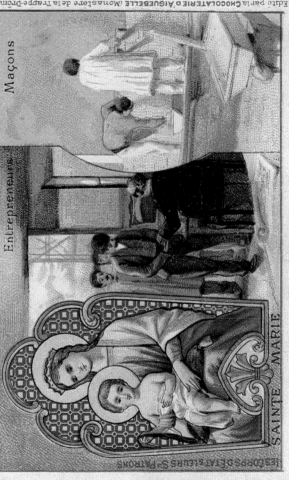

Maçons

Entrepreneurs

SAINTE MARIE

LES CORPS D'ÉTAT & LEURS SᵗˢPATRONS

MIDNIGHT MASS

TRADITIONALLY, THIS WAS THE FIRST OF A SERIES
OF THREE MASSES IN HONOR OF JESUS.

Since the twelfth century, the Catholic Church has celebrated three Masses on Christmas. This came from the pope's obligation to offer Mass at several churches in Rome on that day; Charlemagne extended this practice to his whole empire. The first of these three rites is Midnight Mass, or the Mass of the Angels. It recalls the belief that arose in the thirteenth century according to which Jesus was born at midnight. Custom required that the faithful gather in the night in a torchlight procession. Two more celebrations would follow: the Dawn Mass, or Mass of the Shepherds, and Christmas Day Mass, or Mass of the Divine Word. Since the nineteenth century, the Masses have been celebrated consecutively, but since the 1950s the family holiday celebration has grown to the point that it has eclipsed the religious rite. Today the Midnight Mass takes place earlier and earlier in the evening so that the faithful don't miss the holiday feast and the exchange of gifts on Christmas Eve.

Usages & Costumes d'Alsace

Zinclfewig

MINCEMEAT PIE

This covered tart of dried fruit and spices is known as mincemeat pie because the original recipe included ground meat, usually mutton, or if meat was scarce, suet. Its history began in the eleventh century with the return of Crusaders bringing home spices from the Near East. In homage to the birth of Christ, the pastry originally took the form of a cradle. The filling had to include the three spices that, according to legend, the Three Wise Men brought as gifts for Jesus: cinnamon, clove, and nutmeg. From thatched cottages to the court of England, the mince pie became more and more common on the table at Christmas. In 1657 Oliver Cromwell, self-declared lord protector of the Commonwealth, prohibited the festivities of the end of the year, restricting the enjoyment of mincemeat pie. As soon as Charles II gained the throne in 1660, he re-established the celebration of Christmas, and mincemeat pie returned in triumph. In the twentieth century, it was transformed into a smaller pastry, still indispensible to the holiday menu. On Christmas Eve there are few English children who go to bed without leaving some mince pie out for Father Christmas.

SCÈNES DE NOËL.

VÉRITABLE EXTRAIT DE VIANDE LIEBIG.

LA NOËL EN ANGLETERRE.
Dîner de Noël au commencement du siècle (Plum-Pudding).

Voir au verso.

MISTLETOE

THE CUSTOM OF KISSING UNDER THE MISTLETOE AND MAKING A WISH COMES FROM CELTIC AND SCANDINAVIAN LORE.

In botany, mistletoe—the species *Viscum album* in Europe—is a plant parasite that grows on trees. Unlike its host, it keeps its leaves in winter, when its berries become a translucent white. The Celts considered it a magic and sacred plant for its medicinal qualities. On the first night of the Celtic New Year, called "Mother Night," the Druids dressed in white and went to gather mistletoe with a golden sickle and an immaculate white linen cloth with which to catch it. They would proclaim "O Ghel an Heu!" ("May the corn sprout!"). Ever since those times, mistletoe has been associated with the New Year. According to a Scandinavian legend, the sun god Baldur was killed by Loki with an arrow poisoned with mistletoe (which in high doses is toxic). Preyla, goddess of love, promised that if Baldur were revived she would kiss whoever passed beneath the mistletoe. This legend led to the custom of kissing under the mistletoe while sharing wishes for the New Year as a token of goodwill.

Joyeux Noël.

MRS. SANTA

THE WIFE OF SANTA, ADDED TO FOLKLORE
FAIRLY RECENTLY, REMAINS HAZY.

As Santa Claus gained in popularity in the early twentieth century, his home life was imagined. This quite human and secular character could perfectly well lead an almost ordinary existence. We know that he lives in the North with elves and reindeer and that he has a wife, Mrs. Claus. We've not heard that they have any children. Mrs. Santa is usually depicted as a stout older woman whose only responsibility seems to be taking care of her ample household. Santa Claus doesn't ask her to help deliver gifts. Other women in the world, however, assume this task: the fairy Tante Arie in Franche-Compté in eastern France, the witch Befana in Italy, the young Christkindel in Germany, old Babouschka in Russia, or Saint Lucy in Sweden. Some prefer nevertheless to think of Mrs. Santa and to attribute more common sense to her than to her husband.

Christmas Greetings

THE NATIVITY

THE WORD *NATIVITY*, WHICH MEANS "BIRTH," IS
RESERVED TO DESCRIBE THE BIRTH OF JESUS.

The Gospel according to Luke recounts that Joseph had to go to his birthplace of Bethlehem for the census. He left Nazareth with Mary, who was soon to deliver her child. With nowhere else to stay in Bethlehem, they found shelter in a cave that was used as a stable, and it was there that Jesus was born. The Evangelists do not mention the ox and the ass, but the two do appear in Old Testament prophecies. The first depictions of the Nativity come from the fourth century; over time, other figures show up to complete the scene: the angels, shepherds, and the Magi. The Nativity inspired artists of the Middle Ages in particular. Byzantine iconography favored a family scene, with Mary holding her child in her arms. Western religious art of the Renaissance shows Christ's parents on their knees, adoring their child.

Joyeux Noël

NEW YEAR'S DAY

THE FIRST DAY OF THE YEAR IS CELEBRATED
EVERYWHERE BUT ON DIFFERENT DAYS.

No matter the continent, the culture, or the calendar, human beings have celebrated the New Year ever since they first recognized the cycles of the natural world in the most ancient times. Observances were a matter of greeting the renewal of Nature and its message of hope. Often celebrations would be held on the winter solstice, when day prevails over night, or at the vernal equinox. The date would change in cases of movable calendars, such as the system in ancient Egypt, which was based on the flooding of the Nile, or the Chinese lunar calendar. Religious considerations were also in play: in France, under Charlemagne, the year started on Christmas Day; under the Capetian kings of France, the year started on Easter. Regional traditions sometimes determined the date. In 1564, an edict of Charles IX of France set the observance for his kingdom as January first, the day already favored by the Romans. The pope extended this choice to the entire Catholic world in 1622. New Year's celebrations in most cultures, however, now have no religious connotations. The sole survival of the notion of renewal is that people make their New Year's resolutions.

NEW YEAR'S GIFTS

THIS WAS A PAGAN TRADITION, CONDEMNED BY THE CHURCH, THAT HAS ENDURED THROUGH TIME.

The custom of offering New Year's gifts goes back to ancient Rome. People of high rank were given fragrant branches of vervain gathered from the sacred grove of the beneficent goddess Strenia, from which the French word for New Year's gifts, *étrennes*, derives. Over time the Romans replaced the gifts of Strenia's branches. Sweets and small objects were exchanged among relatives, friends, and neighbors, but influential people received gifts of greater consequence. In Roman times the year began in March; the specific date fluctuated in Europe until 1564, when New Year's was set as the first of January. But neither the changing of dates nor the condemnation of the Church stopped the custom of *étrennes* (in business relations or politics). In 1789 in France, the National Assembly prohibited the practice based on the propensity for corruption but without success; nowadays in France *étrennes* are given to service providers such as mail deliverers, housekeepers, nannies, and firefighters.

PÈRE FOUETTARD (FATHER WHIPPER)

THIS HELPER OF SAINT NICHOLAS, SCARY
AND MENACING, WAS INTENDED TO
FRIGHTEN CHILDREN INTO OBEDIENCE.

Adults used to threaten unmanageable children with the coming of Père Fouettard, or Father Whipper. Yet this dreadful character only came once a year, when he accompanied Saint Nicholas on his rounds on the sixth of December. His appearance inspires immediate panic. Dressed all in black, covered in a big coat and a hood out of which point his horns, he wears heavy boots or wooden shoes whose clatter announces his arrival. Sometimes he has a long tail like the Devil or the attributes of a goat. His tools are no less terrifying: a whip or a bundle of switches with which to chastise disobedient children, and a large sack with which to capture them. In different regions he is given different names. In Alsace, he is called Hans Trapp, inspired by the eighteenth-century Hans von Trotha, a bloodthirsty nobleman. In alpine regions, the shaggy Krampus, a creature with horns and claws, rattles chains and bares his fangs. In Germany, Knecht Ruprecht uses a sack full of ashes to slap children who don't know their prayers. This character moved with German emigrants to Brazil, where they called him Pelznickel. Since the evolution of principles of child rearing, children are free of fear of Père Fouettard. He remains nonetheless a primordial element in Saint Nicholas processions.

REINDEER

RUDOLPH, THE LITTLE REINDEER WITH THE RED NOSE, IS THE MOST FAMOUS OF SANTA'S CREW.

In 1823 the New York pastor Clement Clarke Moore laid the foundation for the future archetype of Santa in his poem "A Visit from Saint Nicholas," also known as "The Night Before Christmas." Moore endowed Santa with eight reindeer: Dasher, Dancer, Prancer, Vixen, Comet, Cupid, Donner, and Blitzen. Later, they were each given a gender and a personality, although Moore had said nothing on this. In 1939 Robert L. May added a new reindeer and named him Rudolph. He wrote jingles for the Montgomery Ward Company, which sold coloring books at Christmastime. Rudolph, shy and sensitive, has a glowing red nose that helps him guide the sleigh. He was a great success. Alas, Mr. May did not obtain a copyright for his creation. He finally did recover rights in 1947. Two years later his brother-in-law composed the song "Rudolph the Red-Nosed Reindeer," which allowed them to live out their days in comfort.

ROBIN REDBREAST

SEVERAL LEGENDS TELL WHY THE ROBIN
IS ASSOCIATED WITH CHRISTMAS.

The European robin, or robin redbreast, often appears on Christmas cards, especially in England. He owes this privilege to a legend. This pretty little bird worked so hard blowing on the fire to stir it and warm the baby Jesus that the heat singed the feathers on his breast and made them red. Another explanation of his link to Christmas comes from the eighteenth century, when English postmen, busier at holiday time when they delivered greeting cards, wore a red cloak that earned them the name redbreast. Provençal tradition suggests another version, a Christmas story that tells how one Christmas Eve, battered by a glacial wind, a robin asked for shelter in a beech tree and then in an oak but was rebuffed. Finally a fir tree opened its branches, and the robin spent a peaceful night. In the morning, he discovered at the foot of the tree a space free of snow where some earthworms wriggled. The famished bird pecked with such ardor that his breast turned crimson, and he sang for joy. As for the fir tree, as a reward for its kindness, it came to be that its foliage would always stay green.

ROCKING THE CRADLE
OF BABY JESUS

THIS FORGOTTEN CUSTOM BID THE FAITHFUL
TO COME CLOSE TO THE CHRIST CHILD.

The custom of rocking the cradle of the baby Jesus (in French, *le bercement de l'enfant Jésus*) was maintained into the eighteenth century in Europe. In life-size village Nativity scenes, or *crèches*, popular since the thirteenth century, a figure of the infant Jesus was placed in a cradle, which each villager by turn could gently rock. The movement was said to soon give the believer a sense of peace conducive to contemplation, in preparation for a worthy welcome for the Christ Child.

Une ancienne coutume de Noël : le bercement de l'Enfant Jésus (Dessin de Damblans)

SAINT NICHOLAS OF MYRE

THE REPUTATION FOR GENEROSITY OF THIS EARLY
CHRISTIAN BISHOP MADE HIM A LEGENDARY FIGURE.

Nicholas of Myre was born into a rich and pious family in Lycia, on the coast of present-day Turkey, in the year 270. According to his legend, as an infant he stood up on the day of his baptism. Ordained as a priest at the age of nineteen, he soon succeeded his uncle as bishop of Myre and became notable for many acts of mercy and generosity, including supporting three young neighbors to help them avoid turning to prostitution for their livelihood. He intervened to save the lives of three of Emperor Constantine's officers who had been unjustly condemned to death, an act that became a popular subject in medieval art and embellished over time. Traditionally depicted in art on a smaller scale than the saint, the soldiers eventually were transformed into three young students. The legend eventually became a tale of Saint Nicholas restoring to life three children killed by a butcher who had salted them in a vat of brine. This story was retold in medieval mystery plays and ballads. Highly popular, celebrations of the feast day of Saint Nicholas on December sixth became a children's festival.

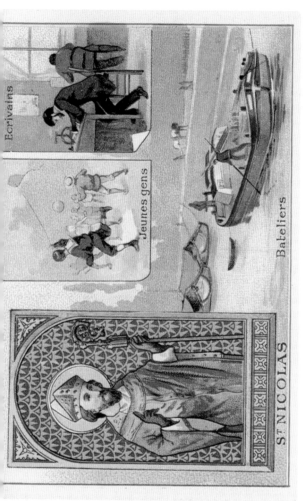

Ecrivains

Jeunes gens

Bateliers

ST NICOLAS

SANTA COCA-COLA

THE MAKER OF SODA POP POPULARIZED THE
RED-AND-WHITE OUTFIT OF SANTA CLAUS.

In the early nineteenth century, Saint Nicholas emigrated to the United States, where he used the name Santa Claus. Around 1850, he began to do the work of Father Christmas, taking presents to children on Christmas Eve. Under the pen of the artist Thomas Nast, he became a rotund, charming old man. Nast, an illustrator for the New York magazine *Harper's Weekly*, painted him dressed in red and white, and confirmed his residence at the North Pole. The celebration of Christmas became increasingly popular, and brands exploited the character in their advertising as of the early twentieth century. Coca-Cola, who adopted the red-and-white Santa, codified his image in a 1931 publicity campaign. The American company wanted to encourage children to drink their beverage in all seasons. The illustrator Haddon Sundblom drew Santa enjoying a Coke before resuming his journey. Some Catholics objected to this misappropriation, but Coca-Cola managed to send the red-and-white Santa around the world thanks to their advertising, and with him the holy day became boldly commercial.

A MERRY Christmas

SANTA'S HOME

SEVERAL COUNTRIES CLAIM THE HONOR OF
BEING THE LOCATION OF SANTA'S HOME.

In the 1850s, the American illustrator Thomas Nast, who had already established his conception of the image of Santa Claus, described this friend of children as living at the North Pole. Finlanders responded in 1927 that this was impossible. They had an unbeatable argument: practically nothing grew at the North Pole; the good fellow wouldn't be able to feed his reindeer there.

The people of Finland said he lived in their country in the land of the Sami people, first at Korvatunturi, then at Rovaniemi. But all the countries with snow-covered territories claimed the residence of Santa. The Swedes placed him at Gesunda, north of Stockholm; the Norwegians at Droeback, south of Oslo; the Danes in Greenland; the Canadians in their Far North. The stakes are high when it comes to tourism.

LA NATURE ET SES MERVEILLES

Aurore boréale (LAPONIE)

SANTA IN THE SOVIET UNION

TO BREAK WITH WESTERN TRADITION
WITHOUT DISHEARTENING CHILDREN, THE
USSR BROUGHT IN FATHER FROST.

Sworn enemy of religion as well as capitalism, the Soviet Union could not condone the celebration of the birth of Christ nor that of Santa Claus, ambassador for the society of consumption and suspected shameless exploiter of elves. But to put it simply, suppressing the joys of Christmas would have been too unpopular. In 1928, the Soviet government found a compromise solution: they reactivated a character from Slavic folklore, Ded Moroz, or Father Frost. This legendary figure had a bad reputation for kidnapping children, whom he would freeze. But in the twentieth century he took on more of the traits of Saint Nicholas: wearing a long blue, white, or red coat and a long beard and driving a horsedrawn troika. He lived in the industrial town of Veliki Oustioug. To stay secular, he traveled on the first of January. He did not give gifts to individuals but to collectives, committees, local councils, or settlements. After 1945, he was adopted outside the USSR in all the Eastern bloc countries and given local nicknames. His Romanian avatar was sometimes depicted as an athletic-looking proletarian worker.

С НОВЫМ ГОДОМ!

SLEIGH

THIS NORDIC MEANS OF TRANSPORT WAS
LINKED TO SANTA BY AN AMERICAN PASTOR.

The poem "A Visit from Saint Nicholas," published in 1823 by the American pastor Clement Clarke Moore, is a landmark in the history of Christmas traditions. In moving the visit of Saint Nicholas from the night of December fifth to the twenty-fourth, the author focused attention on the commemoration of the birth of Jesus. He also sketched out the secular benefactor, the future Santa Claus. The new Saint Nicholas had many similar traits that made him the friend of children. Although of English descent, Moore borrowed Scandinavian traditions to portray this character, such as having his hero travel in a sleigh pulled by reindeer. Expanding his sphere of influence, Santa goes to countries rarely covered in snow in December, so his vehicle has to fly, which leads him to make his deliveries via chimneys. In Holland, Saint Nicholas goes about flying but on a white horse. In most other countries he rides a donkey. For children, it's all the same: they leave a carrot or apple for the animals, without which the much-awaited gifts won't reach them.

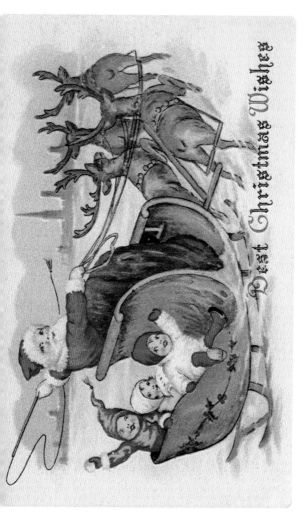

Best Christmas Wishes

SNOW

ALTHOUGH CHRISTMAS SUGGESTS VISIONS
OF SNOW, MOST PEOPLE IN THE WORLD
DON'T SEE IT ON THE APPOINTED DAY.

Many well-known Christmas traditions come from Northern Europe. Father Christmas lives at the North Pole or in Scandinavia, and winter weather in these regions explains the association of snow with Christmas. The symbolism of white in Western cultures joins perfectly with this, evoking purity, chastity, innocence, spirituality, peace. Snow at Christmas crowns the celebration and even serves as a good omen, as expressed in the weather-predicting proverbs "White Christmas, green Easter," or "Snowy Christmas, beautiful spring." As for the snowman, he has been a traditional Christmas tree decoration since the early twentieth century. Most of the children in the world, however, have a slim chance of making a real snowman. In Australia, Brazil, Mali, or Thailand, for example, temperatures approach 86°F in December (30°C). In the Middle East or southern Europe, the thermometer rarely goes below 50°F (10°C), too far from the 32°F (0°C) required for snow crystals to fall.

THE STAR OF BETHLEHEM

THE STAR WAS IN REALITY THE PLANET VENUS, BUT ITS NAME HAS COME THROUGH THE CENTURIES.

The Gospel according to Matthew tells that the Star of Bethlehem guided the Three Wise Men to Bethlehem from the East. But this star was in truth a planet, Venus. Close to the Sun, Venus shines with a special brightness. Following close to the Sun's course, we can't see Venus in the middle of the night, but its extraordinary brilliance is visible at dusk or dawn according to the season. At sunset, Venus marks the west and at daybreak the east. The name Shepherd's Star or *Étoile du berger* came from the planet Venus having served as a compass for shepherds. Knowledge of astronomy would lead us to believe that the Magi, who were coming from Persia, east of Palestine, would have been beckoned by the Star of Bethlehem at nightfall. But no text tells how they found their way in the daylight of the twelve days that tradition says their journey to Bethlehem lasted.

Noël Noël

SWEETS

Many traditional Christmas confections take a symbolic shape, such as the German *Christstollen*, known since the fourteenth century. Oblong and sprinkled with powdered sugar, it is said to symbolize the Christ Child in his swaddling clothes. The loaf made of fruit and nuts contains no eggs, butter, or milk, since in older times the Church forbade their use during the Christmas season. A spice bread with the same sanction on ingredients remains another Christmas tradition in Germany. Many regions of France have traditional Christmas cookies and sweet biscuits: *coigneux* in Vosges, *cochelins* in Beauce, *aguignettes* in Normandy, *naulets* in Berry. Friends and family give these treats as New Year's gifts as well. In the nineteenth century, chocolate, once reserved for the rich, became democratized. In 1895 in southeastern France, the Savoyard pastry chef Louis Dufour invented the chocolate truffle. In the same period, across the Atlantic, a candy maker invented the candy cane. A nonsecular interpretation of this simple, hard sugar candy describes its white color as homage to the virgin birth of the Messiah; its form in the shape of a letter *j* for the initial of Jesus and its red stripes for the flagellation. In modern times, little gourmands can happily eat their candy canes unaware of this last piece of iconography.

CHOCOLAT SUCHARD

Serrières

Cacao · Suchard · Chocolat

TOYS

CHRISTMAS TOYS BECAME A COMMERCIAL
WINDFALL IN THE LATE NINETEENTH CENTURY.

Over the course of the nineteenth century, children became more and more the object of attention, and Christmas would focus on them. The promise of a present encouraged good behavior. Department stores, an invention of the 1850s, were quick to get the hint. Retailers saw that to earn customer loyalty they could renew reasons for shopping by creating "seasons." From early December, they piled shelves with mountains of toys. In 1886, the magazine *L'Illustration* in France released the first special issue on Christmas gifts. The Paris store Bon Marché envisioned the first window display of toys in France in 1893. At the time, children in families of modest means were content to receive candies or, the supreme rare delicacy, an orange. The arrival of Father Christmas in Europe at the beginning of the period of prosperity from 1945 to 1975 democratized the purchase of toys. Advertising proliferated, and toy makers went into fierce competition; children placed their orders for Santa, even when they didn't believe in him anymore, and parents made major financial commitments to satisfy them.

Bonne Année!

TURKEY AND GOOSE

THE TURKEY, IMPORTED FROM AMERICA, DETHRONED THE GOOSE ON THE CHRISTMAS TABLE.

In ancient times, the goose was considered a solar bird, eaten during the festivals celebrating the winter solstice. The tradition was transferred to Christmas on a date chosen by the Church to replace the pagan solstice rites with the Christian holy day. In the sixteenth century, Jesuit missionaries brought a large winged creature back to Europe from the Americas. (When they thought they had landed in the Indies, they named it "chicken of India," a name that eventually contracted to *dinde* in French.) Native Americans, who had domesticated it, also considered the turkey a solar bird and used its feathers to adorn the headpieces worn by their leaders. In Europe this exotic bird held prestige; it was reserved for royal tables and was raised in the zoo at Versailles. It was first served for Christmas at the court of the Holy Roman Emperor Charles VII at the beginning of the seventeenth century. Little by little, the turkey took over except in goose-raising regions such as Alsace or the southwest of France. In the 1930s, producers bred smaller varieties better adapted for families that were becoming smaller, too.

L'Oie de Noël

B. SIRVEN. IMP. EDIT. TOULOUSE - PARIS

VENERATION OF THE INFANT JESUS

THE CARMELITE ORDER, FOUNDED DURING THE
CRUSADES, CONTRIBUTED TO THE SPREAD OF THE
PRACTICE OF VENERATION OF THE INFANT JESUS.

Veneration of the Holy Childhood of Christ, a Catholic devotion, is an invitation to recover the state of innocence of childhood in order to access a pure faith without resistance. The practice began in the seventeenth century, promoted in France by a Carmelite nun, Marguerite de Beaune. A Christian mystic since childhood, at thirteen she declared that she was "the bride of the Holy Child Jesus in the manger," saying that Jesus himself, appearing to her as a nursling, told her this. In 1637 the nun gained fame for having brought about by means of her prayers, according to legend, the birth of the future King Louis XIV. A statue said to have belonged to Saint Teresa of Ávila helped spread this devotion to the Christ Child; donated to a Carmelite monastery in Prague in 1628, the Infant Jesus of Prague is said to have averted many perils. Veneration of the infant Jesus culminated in the nineteenth century. Catholic homes everywhere kept statuettes, sometimes naked, sometimes in swaddling, sometimes sumptuously robed and crowned in imitation of the statue in Prague. Today the Infant Jesus of Prague is kept in the Church of Our Lady of Victory in the Czech capital, where it still attracts pilgrims.

HEUREUX NOËL

M.S.i.B. 13762.

THE WINTER SOLSTICE

ON THE SOLSTICE, IT IS NEARLY UNIVERSAL
TO CELEBRATE THE REBIRTH OF THE SUN.

In the Northern Hemisphere, the shortest day of the year is on the winter solstice. After the solstice, daylight lasts longer each following day. Although the solstice fluctuates, convention puts it at the twenty-first of December. In pagan religions, the winter solstice symbolized the renewal of Nature, which people recognized followed cycles. The solstice was dedicated to the Sun, believed to literally be reborn, an event clearly to be celebrated. The Romans consecrated twelve days of jubilation celebrating the rebirth of the *Sol invictus*, the unconquered sun. Their festivities also honored Saturn, the god of agriculture. The Celts celebrated the solstice, as did the Germanic and Scandinavian peoples, with *Jul* (Yule). Beliefs and rituals varied among regions and cultures, some honoring the dead to not displease them, but usually merriment was meant to reign. In the fourth century, the Church substituted observance of the solstice with celebrations of the birth of Christ. Despite the Christianization of Europe, customs honoring the solstice endure.

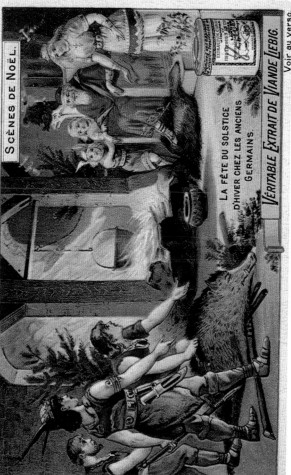

SCÈNES DE NOËL.

LA FÊTE DU SOLSTICE
D'HIVER CHEZ LES ANCIENS
GERMAINS.

VÉRITABLE EXTRAIT DE VIANDE LIEBIG.

Voir au verso.

WOODEN SHOES

IN GERMANY, THE POOR USED TO LEAVE THEIR
WOODEN SHOES OUTSIDE THEIR DOOR TO
COLLECT ANONYMOUS DONATIONS.

Christmas is a time of sharing, when generosity reigns. Thus, when the table is set for Christmas Eve, a place is laid for the first impoverished person who might knock on the door. Custom also called for people of means to make donations to the poor without the recipient's knowing the source. This anonymity contributed to the creation of various legendary personages responsible for giving out gifts to children. Orphans and other unfortunates would not recognize their benefactors. The wooden shoe, or *sabot*, is included among Christmas decorations in memory of this tradition. The custom came from Germany, where the needy would leave their shoes outside their door on Christmas Eve so that the rich could leave their donations, either food or coins, in them. With the introduction of Father Christmas, country children put their wooden clogs on the hearth. When chimneys became as rare as wooden shoes, children put slippers at the foot of the Christmas tree.

Joyeux Noël

OTHER TITLES IN THE SERIES

The Little Book of Saints. Christine Barrely, Saskia Leblon, Laure Péraudin, Stéphane Trieulet. Translated by Elizabeth Bell.

The Little Book of Angels. Nicole Masson. Translated by Elizabeth Bell

The Little Book of Mary. Christine Barrely. Translated by Deborah Bruce-Hostler and Elizabeth Bell.